Writeriffic II

Creativity Training
for Writers

Also by Eva Shaw
from Writeriffic, Inc.

Write Your Book in 20 Minutes [instructional DVD]
Ghostwriting for Fun & Profit
What to Do When a Loved One Dies
Shovel It: Nature's Health Plan

Online Writing Courses*
Taught by Eva Shaw

Writeriffic: Creativity Training for Writers
Writeriffic II: Creativity Training for Writers
Travel Writing
Write Your Life Story
The Craft of Magazine Writing

*Thousands have become published (and best-selling) authors after taking these fast-paced, economical courses, available via Education To Go (www.ed2go.com) and through your local colleges and universities worldwide.

Writeriffic II

Creativity Training
for Writers

Eva Shaw, Ph.D.

Writeriffic Inc.
760-434-6445 [for orders: 866-244-9047]
PO Box 524
Carlsbad CA 92018-0524
www.writeriffic.com

Cover design, interior design/typesetting: Teri Rider, www.teririder.com
Photo credit: CeCe Canton, www.cecephoto.com

Printed in the United States of America

Eva Shaw. – 1st ed.
p. cm.
ISBN: 978-0-9705758-6-9

1.Authorship. 2.Creation (Literary, artistic, etc.) I. Title.

Writeriffic® is a registered trademark.

Dedication:

To Rosy Geranium,
who is good inside and out, because to paraphrase Groucho Marx:
Outside of a dog, a writer's best friend is a book.

Table of Contents

Meet Your Mentor

Look for the word *prolific* in a dictionary, and one of the definitions will be Eva Shaw. Check *best-selling* and *award winning*, too. You'll see Eva's name there as well.

As an author and ghostwriter, she has produced more than seventy books, which have garnered rave reviews and won prestigious awards. Her articles have appeared in those national magazines you see at the supermarket and scores of others. At last count, she has produced more than two thousand articles. With this impressive publishing record, some writers might slow down. Not Eva. New books are underway and articles are being published monthly.

Eva is a lively, engaging, and highly sought-out mentor and speaker. At conferences and events throughout the United States, her presentations draw standing-room-only crowds who seek her advice on writing and publishing. Unlike other well-published writers, Eva happily shares the tricks of the trade and how you, too, can become as abundantly creative. With the sure-fire steps she outlines, every writer can be published.

Thousands have taken her writing classes, and they are living their dreams. They are published writers because they have taken Eva's advice, read her books on writing, watched her instructional DVD, *Write Your Book in 20 Minutes*, and enrolled in her courses. They have asked for mentoring, and she's lavished them with her tips, tools, and tricks of the trade.

Eva teaches writing with Education To Go, www.ed2go.com, and her unbeatable online classes are so popular that they are offered at two thousand colleges and universities worldwide. The courses are Travel Writing, The Craft of Magazine Writing, Write Your Life Story, and the highly popular Writeriffic: Creativity Training for Writers, with its second part, Writeriffic: Advanced Creativity Training for Writers (perfect for focused wordsmiths).

Eva says, "I want to hear your stories and your successes. Write to me at askeva@evashaw.com or P. O. Box 524, Carlsbad, CA 92018-0524."

How to Use Writeriffic

Would an athlete enter a marathon without first becoming fit? Would a hopeful singer head to a once-in-a-lifetime audition without taking voice lessons? What about an emerging writer?

Are you trying to jump into the writing world without training? How prepared are you for the competitive world of writing?

To be inventive and increase creativity, we need to write and train in order for our skills to be sharpened. That's what this book is about. It's filled with tips on creativity and training assignments to improve your creative work and even help get you over that bugaboo, writer's block.

In this book you'll find the insider school stuff you need. The material shares the information on creativity and writing that I've gathered in my twenty-plus years as a professional writer and in the last twelve years teaching online as I've mentored thousands of emerging writers. You'll discover in these pages:

- How to increase self-confidence.

- How to boost your creative gifts.

- How to capture your writer's voice and make it sing.

- How to create a creative lifestyle that promotes innovation.

- How to overcome the fear of starting.

- How to know you have what it takes to be a writer.

- And scores of writing tricks.

I believe that because of your life's experiences, you have a natural talent to write. Every person can write. Sometimes we don't get the right kind of creative support from family and friends. It's a truism. But here in this book you can write, reflect, and practice the craft of writing. When the time is right, you'll be able to seek publication because you will know you're ready. How so? Every writing assignment will be a reflection on where you are with your writing skill at that time. Each time you review your writing in this journal/workbook, you'll see progress.

I have created the Writeriffic assignments for you, and I hope you'll consider me your mentor, as if I were sitting with you or you and I were in a classroom.

This book and its assignments are guaranteed to boost your creativity. When you flip through the pages, you might initially think that the assignments look easy. Do not be fooled. They are deceptively simple. The assignments will take you five minutes or five hours. It's up to you. Most of the assignments include variations that can become a part of a long-term creativity program. Yes, you have the potential right in your hands to create a once-a-day writing program that could last a year or more.

Turn to the assignments and look at the blank pages next to them. You'll use these to complete the assignments. See the words "Continued on page ___" at the bottom of each page? Should you need more than one page to complete the exercise, there are pages at the back of the book. Simply fill in the appropriate page number, and you can instantly find the continuation of your writing.

I've created assignments for this book that are not in any other program, workshop, or classroom. These are brand-new assignments.

With the writing assignments in the first edition of this book, writers learned to capture their creative voice. Some took the assignments, turned them into short stories, essays, and novels and went on to have the work published. Will that happen with you and these new assignments? I hope so. I've seen it happen with other writers I've mentored, so why not with you?

That's it. Use this book. Make it your new best friend, and it will be. Good writing.

Escape the Fear

What frightens you? Speaking in front of large groups? Walking on coals? The all-you-can-eat-half-price sushi buffet? Okay, seriously, who hasn't looked at a blank computer screen or a sheet of paper and gotten the willies? Real writers get "page fright," too, you know.

When you glare at that page, what happens? Does it glower? Intimidate you? Have you ever wondered what you could or should write? Have you ever stopped writing?

This is a serious disease for writers. Page fright has ended the career of gifted wordsmiths. It's worse than writer's block, which can often be cured with rest, a bit more research, and a personal pep talk.

Every day, we writers stare at the blank screen or lined tablet. I have been troubled by the ailment more than once in my writing career. I've learned ways to get over it. You can do it, too, once you have the tools. Then you can become the creative, resourceful, happy, and clever novelist, nonfiction writer, short-story writer, storyteller, poet, screenwriter, or playwright you've dreamed of becoming.

Before you let page fright trip you, consider the other things that might be going on in your life that may be stopping you from writing. This doesn't mean you're a failure by any stretch of the imagination. It assures me that you're a bona fide human being.

Let's say that you've been given a critical project that's going to demand hours of overtime, the kids or pets or parents are at a troubling time in their lives, the car made a weird noise on the way to the office, and your throat feels scratchy. Yes, I've had times, heck, years like that myself. That's where these assignments can be a lifesaver, a creative port in the storm. Even on the most hectic of days, when chaos fills the air as thick as smog in LA, if you do one or two of the assignments, you can break through and out of the smog, um, I mean, fright. You can breathe in creativity and work on your craft.

If page fright hits, look at what's happening in your nonwriting life, your work life, and your relationships. Are you getting enough sleep? Do you need to talk with your doctor or a listening friend? Is it time to sharpen your computer skills or learn researching techniques? There could be lots of reasons why you're suffering, and they all could be because life sometimes gets in our way.

For the next few minutes, pretend a large box with a sturdy lid is sitting next to you. Take the lid off, and imagine you're jamming in all your favorite reasons and problems and excuses for not writing. You can even pretend that a complaining loved one, a boss, or a co-worker is going inside. Put in the ones about being a "bad" writer, not having a degree in journalism, or being forced to write without a rich relative to support you while you concentrate on creativity.

Now slam that lid closed. Put a heavy book on top if that makes the box more secure. Don't let those problems or excuses out for the next six weeks or while you're doing the Writeriffic assignments. If you ever want them, they'll be there. Actually, after you've finished the assignments you might try those problems on for size. I have a hunch that you won't want them anymore as accessories to your confident and resourceful creative life.

Don't you feel more creative already?

Now that you're open to a more creative life, let's talk about the nature of creativity. Forget what someone once wrote or said about good writers having to "open a vein." Sorry, I'm not willing to bleed for my work and would never expect you to, either. Besides, that concept is downright messy.

Writing is Fun. Really.

You'll get an earful if you ask twenty civilians, that is, nonwriters, how one should write and what's the trick to becoming more creative. Negative folks will tell you that creativity cannot be taught. If you don't have it, you can't get it. Know-it-alls will tell you it's so easy. But the truth is that learning to be a creative writer takes time and practice. It's really fun, too. Regardless of your age or your background, you can be a published writer.

I must admit that once you catch the exhilaration, the pure bliss of creativity and writing, you'll become addicted. But don't worry. This addiction is good for you.

Creativity is as invigorating as a walk through the countryside on a perfect spring day. Creativity is like winning an unexpected prize, getting into those jeans you wore in high school, being told that your house or car is worth twice as much as when you bought it years ago, and seeing a toddler take a first step. Creativity is these feelings all rolled into one.

You may already be writing or have a desire to write fiction—to tell stories for novels or short stories. You may be composing poetry, concocting images that are thoughtful and dazzling. You may be writing articles or nonfiction books and need to enliven the text to make them irresistible. Or you may be thinking of writing the stories of your life or the lives of those folks you love.

Yet, you may also realize that your creative skills aren't as good as you would like. That's not being negative, but smart. Like the training athletes and singers require, which I mentioned in the beginning, writing takes practice, and practice takes time.

Did you just think, "How does Eva know this?" I've made choices in my own career to design and live a creative life, and without a doubt I know there's a more creative life waiting for you. But you must take that first step. You must read this book and do the assignments. When you do, you'll never look back and wonder, "Could I have been a good writer?" You'll be a good writer, with practice.

Being a creative writer means honoring your creative feelings. You'll need to pull ideas from deep inside or straight from this morning's newspaper. You must feed, nourish, and nudge that creative energy, encourage it to blossom, to take chances and to grow. If creative writing were a garden, you'd need to water, tend, and make sure it has sunlight. I'm an avid gardener, so pardon my metaphors, but you get the idea. Cultivate the creative life. Make being creative a choice.

Creativity means you need to filter or sift through the thoughts coming from your head and the everyday world. There are some well-meaning folks, possibly in your close family, who do not understand or like the creative process or creative people. You might not be able to cover your ears when they try to tell you what a futile career or hobby writing is ... but you can reason how you truly feel about writing. Creative writers examine their ideas with their hearts as well as their heads. Yes, this takes practice, but please be assured that you can do it.

Your Writer's Voice

In the writing classes you've taken from me or other writing instructors, you have heard the term *writer's voice*. You do have a unique voice, a way of writing about a topic or telling a story, even if you have yet to hear it.

Think for a moment about a friend or colleague who has a distinctive sound to his or her voice. A Texas twang with you'alls aplenty? An Irish brogue as thick as butter on crusty soda bread? One that shouts, "I'm from the Bronx"? Pretend for a moment that you were going to interview this person for an article. It would be nearly impossible to tell your reader about the friend from Dallas without mentioning her accent, or the man from Dublin and not comment on the lilt of his voice.

But how does one begin to hear and then cultivate a writer's voice? It's part of the evolution of a writer. The more you write, especially in a certain genre, the more you'll find that you're using similar sentence structure, adjectives, and adverbs that feel the same. This doesn't mean that your writing will be boring. On the contrary, you'll soon hear (if you're listening to your words as you read out loud) a rhythm or beat to your prose. (By the way, prose here means any writing. Please don't misunderstand and think I mean poetry.)

My writing is upbeat. It has a *can do* feeling about it. I hope you've felt that in what you've read so far.

I might use this same voice when writing how-to books, self-help books (today also called *prescriptive nonfiction*), and articles, such as, "Yes, you can build a gazebo in a weekend, and here's how." Or, "10 Ways to Teach Teens Thrift." If I were to write a romance novel, I would use another voice, one not quite so chipper and optimistic. If I were to write a horror novel, à la Stephen King, you can bet I would work to scare the reader on the first page. There's nothing upbeat about fear.

Therefore, the more you write in your genre, or many genres, the more practice you'll have at writing in specific ways and hearing the voice that comes from your writing. But—yes, there's usually a "but," isn't there?—you must write and read in your genre.

The writing part is self-explanatory. The more you write, the easier it becomes to format ideas in your head and then allow them to flow to a computer screen or paper. Yet writing teachers often overlook asking the emerging writers in their courses to read. I've never figured out why.

If you're hooked on romance novels, then try your hand at that genre. If it's reading a pithy essay that really makes your day, then head in that direction. Passionate about cars, crankshafts, and carburetors? You'll want to read automobile magazines, and you probably already know the specific buzzwords used, the ones you'll use when writing for the pubs (that is, publications, not taverns).

Unless you read a genre that you're thinking of writing in, you cannot begin to use words and sentences and format ideas in a way that readers of the genre expect. Many emerging writers have told me, "But I want my writing to be special, so everything needs to be different." That's great, but before you can dash off (writing-wise) in an innovative direction, you've got to know the customary way a genre is created.

That's it. Read in your genre. If you don't have a clear idea of the genre in which you want to specialize, then read many different genres. Your brain and heart will direct you.

Recently, in one of my traditional workshops on a college campus, there was an accountant (let's call him "Bud") who felt he must only spend time writing if he could create something important. His desire, he said, was to write The Great American Novel, along the lines of *Atlas Shrugged*, by Ayn Rand, or *The Great Gatsby*, by F. Scott Fitzgerald. But, as Bud admitted, he really hadn't enjoyed English Lit in college and only got by because he used *CliffsNotes*. He never read the classics, and yet Bud spent about seven years agonizing over an attempt to become Hemmingway, minus the addiction to alcohol and dangerous living. When he arrived in my course, he was an unhappy camper. We talked about genre, and I asked a simple question. It's the same question I'm asking you right now.

What do you like to read when you read for fun?

Bud's answer was cookbooks and mysteries. He gobbled up cookbooks like some folks munch M&M's and was an enormous fan of the amateur detective along the lines of Dorothy Sayer's Lord Peter Wimsey. You probably already get my suggestion, and that's exactly what I recommended to Bud. Write a mystery where the protagonist is a chef, a caterer, a great cook in the evenings and an accountant by day. Suddenly he couldn't stop smiling; he'd found his genre, and the ideas poured in quicker than he could write them down.

You do not have to make a decision on your genre today or even for a few months. Actually, I would prefer you didn't typecast yourself. I hope you'll take risks writing these assignments. Why not stretch yourself and try some genres that you haven't considered before. You can make this easy and settle for what you've been writing for a long time or, like Bud, you can take a chance. Remember, this is school, and you're here to learn. You can do the assignments over and over. You can skip assignments that just don't click with your creative self. However, if you skip assignments, consider returning to them once you've built up more creative writing muscles by working on the other assignments.

This is not a Writeriffic assignment. You'll have plenty of those. I would like you to create a pile in your office, bedroom, or kitchen of books or magazines that you want to read—then dig into them.

Your Inner Writer

I'm often asked, Is it possible to turn our creative visions, even those that haven't taken form yet, into purposeful prose? You bet—and then some.

Those who are just testing the waters of creative writing sometimes think that the ideas that come out of nowhere are silly, stupid, or worthless. Yet the more we talk to other writers, the more we realize the stuff that creativity is made of is produced from the visions in our minds. That's pretty remarkable.

Creativity is the way you translate what you hear or feel or see inside into a format that you share with the reader. For writers, creativity is ideas processed into words.

If I were a brain specialist instead of a writer, I could tell you exactly what hormones or brain connections are activated in the creative process. For me, the process doesn't matter as much as how I get those ideas onto the page. We do that with practice.

Do you remember as a youngster learning a new skill? Do you recall learning to ride a bike, play a sport, or dance a complex routine? How about when you learned to maneuver through a favorite video game? Do you remember learning to tie your shoes or shoot baskets? These skills took tenacity and a willingness to make mistakes and take risks throughout the process.

I don't know about you, but when I learned to roller-skate, I wore off the skin on my knees and still got up to try again. I never once wondered whether I was going to wear those pavement-induced scars for the rest of my life. I was determined to skate with the other kids, and I did what it took. Luckily my mother had lots of adhesive bandages.

We had fun learning those skills. That's what creating is about. What feels good to your ear when reading your writing out loud, what makes your heart swell, and what simply makes sense—these become creative visions to share.

Think of writing and creativity as recess for the brain. Not every creative thought must be attached to a novel, short story, poem, essay, book, or article. Not every creative effort must be connected with writing at all. I believe that the more other creative activities you participate in, from painting a barn to painting a picture, the more creative you become and the better your writing will be. You might say that doing any creative activity supports your inner writer.

Right now, take a moment to figure out ways to add more creativity to your world. I love to garden, and if you were to visit my yard right now you would see I'm a creative gardener. When I'm working on a knotty piece of plotting or mulling over research for a nonfiction book, I head for the garden to cut, shovel, and water. Novelist Irving Stone said, "When I have trouble writing, I step outside my studio into the garden and pull weeds until my mind clears—I find weeding to be the best therapy there is for writer's block." No matter what you've heard, it's simply not true that I allow the weeds to grow so I can pull them when I'm having a writing problem.

Here's a start-up list of creative activities to get you going. Notice that they have nothing to do with writing. Make it your goal to add at least one of these activities to your week. Better yet, add one to each day.

- Weaving

- Model making

- Working (in an enjoyable way) on the car

- Craft making

- Playing a musical instrument

- Woodworking and building

- Sewing or other needlecrafts

- Gardening

- Attending a book signing or literary event

- Going to the theater

- Painting

- Yarn crafting

- Singing

- Working with clay

- Baking

- Dancing

- Cooking (but only if you love it)

- Doing puzzles

- Practicing yoga or a stretching routine

- Doodling

- Walking, running, swimming, cycling

As you add more creativity to your life, you will become a more creative writer. It sounds simple because it is.

Becoming a Writer

Did you hear about the person who waited for inspiration? That's right. He was a waiter and not a writer.

What does it take to become a writer? To be a writer, you must write. Are you aware that your writing will never be as incredible as you "heard it" in your head? That's the plight of writers, but we can make it good enough. For the next six weeks (because it takes six weeks for anything to become a habit), I want you to do the following:

- Strive to write every day. Even if you barely have five extra minutes before your eyes fall shut, the baby cries, or your bus drops you off near the office, write. Use the Bubble Method, too! Make it a goal to incorporate writing into your life. You know when you have a few spare minutes, when you can delegate a job, or even when you can forego a task. Find the time if writing is important.

- Look at every relationship and situation in your life as potential for a story, book, article, or essay. A friend, "Joan," is an award-winning writer, and I adore her. But every time we have coffee or dinner, I have the feeling that she's mentally taking notes, and something quirky or weird that's happened in my life will end up in one of her amazing short stories. Ironic, isn't it? Joan's habit of using her family and friends in her own writing has just become part of mine. Writing is like that.

- Start and maintain a clipping file of articles from magazines or newspapers that inspired your creativity. Sebastian Junger was inspired to write the best-selling *Perfect Storm* from seeing the angry Atlantic and keeping a clipping from a newspaper. If something tickles your fancy or brain, cut it out and put it in a file.

- Keep a writing journal on your computer. Or start writing in a spiral notebook. Jot down ideas and tidbits of conversation that you've heard. Ideas are everywhere, from an eavesdropped conversation in the checkout line of the grocery store to a song on the oldies channel that sparks your imagination as you drive to work. Become a gatherer of ideas.

- Don't censor yourself or your writing, including that which you write in your journal. I always tease emerging writers in my traditional writing classes that if they need someone to trash their work, I know people who would love to do so. Seriously? For the next six weeks, don't allow your internal critic (that ugly voice inside your head that says you're silly to write) to speak. It's going to be tough because in about four weeks our "honeymoon" will wear thin, and the critic will begin whispering, "You're a fool to write. You're too old to learn to write. You're too young to write. You're too …" Well, you get the picture, and you may have heard the voice or voices before. Just shh 'em.

- To write, you need the implements of a writer. Carve out a location, and negotiate with your family to spend time at the computer. Friends and family know that if they call after eight-thirty in the evening and want me to do something, I must write myself a note or I won't remember. This has nothing to do with dementia, but rather I'm already shutting down my brain after a long workday of writing and teaching. But if you call at five in the morning, consider it done.

Do the assignments found in this book just as if you were in one of my classes. You can do an assignment a day or just write on the weekend. Remember, you're not aiming for the most grammatically correct piece of prose. Your goal is to become more creative. My colleague, my favorite editor and fellow online writing teacher Jackie Landis says, "Perfection is the enemy of done." Don't strive for perfection. Make a goal to do the assignments.

Are You Fit to Write?

Creativity, to be channeled into writing, must have a direction. You can set up official-sounding goals and objectives, but all I'm asking is that you write every day.

Just ten minutes, or the time it takes to do one of the Writeriffic writing assignments. Don't worry if your writing feels stiff. It's okay. By the time you've written on all the pages in this book, your creative muscles will be strong and powerful. Remember, the more you write, the easier it will become, much like starting a new fitness program and then getting settled into that routine.

Moreover, are you aware that if you start today and write one page every day for just one year, you'll have a piece of work that is 365 pages long? Now let's flip that coin. What if you don't write? Next year, you'll still be thinking that you want to write but have nothing to show for it. Pretty sad picture, isn't it?

Write every day regardless of how you feel or what's going on in your life. Set the kitchen timer or the alarm on your watch. Sit there for five minutes (or longer, depending on your schedule).

Start here in this journal/workbook. Give it a name. Write the name inside the cover. Make it your best friend. Take it to lunch. Seriously, drag it along when you're going on break, heading on a trip, taking a holiday, lounging at the beach, sitting in the garden.

In six weeks, and as you do these assignments, you can reflect back and see your progress. You'll have written proof that you're a better writer.

Hook Your Readers with Your Writing

In conversations and the lessons in other courses that I teach, I've often discussed, dissected, and encouraged you and your peers to create hooks, the vehicle that draws in the reader. Recently I began thinking, "What makes a good hook for me?" We're all different, thank heavens, or life would be boring, so my good hooks might not be yours. The definition of a hook is a writing technique used to grab a reader, to get his or her attention. Hooks are usually in the first sentence of an article or the first paragraph of a short story or book. I researched hooks and found that they must snag my attention almost immediately or I will not spend time reading the work of writing. How about you?

Here are examples that work for me. You may want to consider these and others that have hooked you. Why did they hook or not hook you? Why not take a few minutes at your next writing session to write about what hooks you.

From *Where the Heart Is:*

Novalee Nation, seventeen, seven months pregnant, thirty-seven pounds overweight—and superstitious about sevens, shifted uncomfortably in the seat of the old Plymouth and ran her hands down the curve of her belly.

From *Word Freak:*

The cops arrive, as they always do, their Aegean blue NYPD cruiser bumping onto the sidewalk and into the northwest corner of Washington Square Park.

From *Cliff Walk:*

I made my confession to a rich woman this week.

From Dodie Smith's *I Capture the Castle:*

I write this sitting in the kitchen sink. That is, my feet are in it; the rest of me is on the draining-board, which I have padded with our dog's blanket and the tea-cozy. I can't say that I am really comfortable, there is a depressing smell of carbolic soap, but this is the only part of the kitchen where there is any daylight left. And I have found that sitting in a place where you have never sat before can be inspiring—I wrote my very best poem while sitting on the hen-house. Though even that isn't a very good poem. I have decided my poetry is so bad that I mustn't write any more of it.

From Mitchel Whitington's *Uncle Bubba's Chicken Wing Fling:*

Uncle Bubba was dead. At least, I figured that he would be as soon as Aunt Irma caught up with him.

Note: All of these first paragraphs made me want to know more. They don't shout, but there's the intrigue of why the author is sitting on the sink, why Aunt Irma is after Uncle Bubba, why the police have come, what kind of confession took place, and most seriously, what pickle the protagonist Novalee was in.

The hook may be the most important part of our writing. Those who have taken my online courses of Travel Writing or The Craft of Magazine Writing may remember that one of the assignments was to identify the hooks in articles that we read from *Reader's Digest*.

Why not take some time to reread the books and articles you've enjoyed and ponder why the hooks work. You might want to flip to one of the lined pages in the back of this book and copy out some of your favorite hooks. In one of the assignments you'll find in this book, you'll be asked to brainstorm hooks, so you might want to study a bit on what pulls you in to read published writing.

An Inspired Existence Made Easier

Writers, athletes, and actors have a lot in common. Most writers have rituals that we follow to help us cope with the nervous tension that can come before, during, or even after a writing project is finished. To get on the stage or the playing field, or hit the **Save** key and keep your writing, you may have to go through specific actions.

I've found it intriguing that most writers, including those whose names are on the lists of best-selling books, have rituals they must do before starting. One writer I know must complete six pages of a novel before she stops for the day, but before she gets this far, she has a cup of tea on her patio, reads the paper (comics first), and then takes a long walk.

Another writer likes to get the house in shape before he starts writing. He does the chores, packs lunches for the kids, and waves good-bye to his spouse before knuckling down to the keyboard and his weekly column. "If I don't do all these, I feel guilty," he says, "and my writing is stiff."

A third author starts the writing day by sitting in front of her computer, before turning it on, to ask God for direction in her writing ministry.

I'd like to suggest a ritual I've found helpful. Once I hit the Start button on the computer, I begin my day by saying thank you to someone for something. Although these days I often use e-mail to write notes, I frequently make time to write and send a pretty card. We all love getting postal mail—most of the time the carrier just delivers bills.

Sometimes I'm asked how I have so many people to thank. The card or e-note is really an excuse to get my creative juices flowing and my brain back to thinking in words. I thank family for just being there, friends for putting up with my creative jaunts into whimsy or worse, editors for being kind to my work, agents for responding to my e-mail, colleagues for listening to my newest, craziest schemes. I also write fan letters to my favorite authors, and many of them reply.

Thanking others is a positive, productive way to start a writing time. If you have yet to find a routine, a ritual for yourself, I recommend this one.

Don't think you're strange if you must go through a specific set of movements or rituals before settling down to write. Have you ever seen an actor do deep breathing assignments or a singer warm up her or his voice? What of athletes? We've all seen them pull an ear, yank on a jersey, or touch a good-luck charm. If any of these things work for you, you'll be in good company with others in competitive and creative fields.

Creative Kick Starts

Do you know it's okay to not clean up your desk and put everything in order at the end of your writing time?

Have you ever stopped writing midsentence when you're finished for the day?

These techniques could increase your creativity. Contrary to what some ultraorganized folks think, adding these two techniques to your creative writing tool belt may make a difference in your productivity. I call these Creative Kick Starts.

"Why? How come?" I can almost hear you ask. It's simple.

Those who follow this practice have an edge because when they return, they just pick up where they left off. This is a technique I use all the time, so if you should visit my office, don't just assume I'm messy. The clutter is planned. I don't organize and really clean up until the project on which I'm working is finished.

Using this technique, you really don't stop for the day or stop the writing project. You're just taking a break from it, so it's easier to begin again.

You can also reduce the hurdle of starting any writing project once you realize that many writers share the same fear. We ask ourselves:

What if I can't complete the short story?

What if a reviewer doesn't like my work?

What if I'm not good enough to write another cookbook?

If you could listen inside the fear area of a writer's brain, you would probably hear one of these.

You would hear the fears in my mind, too. Every single time I begin a new writing project, I have a period of worry, misgiving and, okay, alarm. What if, after seventy-plus books and more than two thousand columns and articles, I really can't research, can't compose a sentence, can't finish what I've been contracted to do? Horror of horrors, what if I suddenly can't write?

That's the worry I go through. At one time, fear paralyzed me for weeks. Then with plenty of self-talk (encouraging words spoken out loud and in a commanding voice), I got going. Of course, everything was fine, but it was scary nonetheless.

Now I realize that the feeling of fear is part of my creative process. If you have it, remember it doesn't mean you're a failure or a bad writer—it means you're normal with normal anxieties.

Are You Made of the Write Stuff?

It's a corny title, but you immediately got the picture. That's what writing does. So, how about if we examine that question. Oh, how easy it would be for me to blithely assure you that you really can do this. You can become the writer of your dreams. You'll freelance up a storm, and everything you touch will be snapped up by hungry editors. Your novel will be discovered in the slush pile of manuscripts that often litters editors' offices. Your nonfiction book will create a stir, and every household around the world will buy one.

I could promise all that, but it would not be true.

Writers write. They write when they're feeling good, and they write when they're feeling crummy. They write when they're children; they write when they're old. They write when they're happy and on top of the world. And they write when the rug has been pulled out from under them. The irony here is that most writers, the ones who are committed to their craft, often find that the writing they've done while they're out of sorts (and in, perhaps, a major blue funk) sounds as good in the final, polished draft as the words they have penned when they haven't struggled at all.

Here are some of my all-time favorite writing fallacies.

Fallacy #1: You Must Have Advanced Degrees in Writing to Be a Good Writer

Truth: Read *Life Is So Good* (Random House, 2000). In this remarkable book, author George Dawson, a 103-year-old slave's grandson who learned to read at age ninety-eight, reflects on his life and offers valuable lessons in living and a fresh, firsthand view of America during the twentieth century. What sustained him through the severity of seven decades, with jobs as varied as breaking horses, driving spikes for the railroads, building levees on the Mississippi, and laboring on farms and in sawmills? The message that "life is so good. I do believe it's getting better."

Also look at *Any Given Day: The Life and Times of Jessie Lee Brown Fouveaux*, by Jessie Lee Brown Fouveaux (Warner Books, 1997). Born in 1899, Jessie Lee Brown Fouveaux started writing when she was eighty, as a new college student. In her memoir written late in life, she recalls traveling by a horse-drawn wagon one cold Thanksgiving, with hot rocks and hay placed under the blankets. Her description of all-day laundry routines will make modern folks grateful for their washers and dryers. Fouveaux's account of a bad marriage and the struggle to raise her eight children has the same immediacy and vigor as her childhood memories. Begun as a gift to her grandchildren, this charming text speaks to all readers of the grace and nobility crafted from an ordinary life. It may have been ordinary to Ms. Fouveaux, but it's extremely extraordinary to all her readers.

Sure, there are thousands of educated men and women who write and even more writers who have graduated from the school of experience. Do not buy into the myth that you must have degrees from the best colleges and universities to become a published, yes, even best-selling author. You must have the ability to see things in special ways and then translate, or write down, those things.

Fallacy #2: You Must Have Unlimited, Uninterrupted Time to Write

Truth: One of my friends grew up in a mining town in Kentucky. To escape a horrific family life, she married at fifteen, had three babies in three years, and was deserted by her alcoholic husband in downtown Atlanta one afternoon in July. I met her in a writing class and knew little about her past. I only knew that during the day she worked for the Department of Motor Vehicles and had kids in college. She was finishing her degree, too, and took other classes at night. As we became friends, I learned she wrote in the evenings when she wasn't in school. Not too long ago, I heard through a mutual friend that she'd received a contract from Simon & Schuster, a major publishing house, for a novel loosely based on her life. This was a first novel by an unknown novelist and garnered a $50,000 advance.

John Grisham wrote his first two novels while he was working full time as an attorney and serving in the Mississippi state legislature. Agatha Christie wrote a dozen mysteries while working full time in a hospital during WWII. Margaret Edson wrote the Pulitzer Prize-winning play *Wit* when she got off work at a bicycle shop. Sue Grafton, famous for the ABC series of murder mysteries, said she made the best use of her time while raising two kids and working full time.

I am not only your writing mentor, but I also lecture at workshops and universities. I write articles and essays and at least two books yearly. I ghostwrite for clients. I'm a columnist for an e-zine (an electronic magazine). I have a busy home life, a wonderful family, church responsibilities, and volunteer projects underway. I love to garden, travel, crochet, do crafty projects, make cards, take classes, and read.

Few writers I know have unlimited, uninterrupted time to write. I believe that, at least for some of us, if we did, we'd probably squander it away. Knowing that I have only two hours or maybe three to work on a manuscript that's burning to be completed really puts time into focus.

Grafton said that when her children had grown and the nest was empty, she wasted time. She said, "Now I can write all day long, and I can't get anything done ... I think a full-time job is a blessing."

Food for thought? It's a meal you may want to review a few times when there are four zillion pulls on your writing time.

Fallacy #3: Writing Will Change a Person

Truth: It's long been thought true that writing can change people for the worse. If you write, will you become like Hemingway or a few others and die prematurely? Will you become pompous and wear smoking jackets with leather on the elbows? Will you think depressing thoughts and write about dark, dangerous subjects? Or become so rich and famous that you'll forget the little people, such as co-workers, family, and friends, once you make the big time? Will you fail?

Some people believe that writing will change them in ways that will make them social or familial outcasts. Yes, some of us writers are quirky people. But the truth is that 98 percent of us quirky types were a bit out of the ordinary to start with. Writing for a living, or even writing part time, doesn't change our character. It doesn't force anyone to drink, do drugs, or get caught up in a wild Hollywood lifestyle. Sure, we can choose to become those things, but please don't blame it on writing.

Fallacy #4: You Must Suffer for Your Art

Truth: A few years ago, in my traditional creative writing course on the university campus, Carrie, one of my students, caught up with me as I was walking toward the classroom. "Eva, I'm confused," she began. "You've been the instructor in this class for nine weeks so far, and I don't understand it. I've heard that writers must suffer for their art, must live desperate lives in order to write. This scares me."

I still smile when I think of this bright woman so tormented by a fallacy that many still believe. I stopped right there in the hall and said, "Listen, do I look like I am suffering? No, of course not." While my childhood wasn't close to *Father Knows Best*, it definitely wasn't *The Munsters*, either. I've experienced the normal ups and downs of life that anyone over the age of thirteen knows about.

As I put my books and briefcase on a table in the classroom, Carrie and I talked some more. Pretend you were sitting there with us, because we chatted about how too many emerging writers buy into this myth.

I said, "There are far more writers who are happy, contented, tax-paying, family people than those who live in a musty garret with no insulation in the walls. Think of Mary Higgins Clark, Debbie Macomber, John Grisham, Jan Karon, Amy Tan, and a slew of others. These are normal people with the conventional challenges of life who have made it big-time. Sure, we've all read about the rags-to-riches stories of writers like Stephen King and the late Frank McCourt, who both overcame tremendous adversity to enjoy fame and fortune.

"No. Suffering doesn't guarantee you'll be a great or famous writer. Writing makes you a writer. The more you write, the better writer you'll become."

Fallacy #5: Only Writers Who Are Sure They Can Do It, Succeed

Truth: Oh my, no! If this were the case, few of the hundreds of writers I've met and thousands I've mentored would have not even tried. Those wannabe writers, the ones who only talk about writing and never really write, don't have fears. Why? You've got it. They never get to the middle of a writing project ... because they never start to write.

Fear can be good for us. It keeps us going. It makes us know we're alive. It affirms that we're doing something edgy, something that most people never do. We're creating with words.

The next time you get the willies and think you cannot go on writing, please think about what life would be without it. No writer is sure that he or she will create marketable writing until the writing is completed. That's the truth. Every time we put our fingers to the keyboard or pen to paper, we're taking a chance. There are no guarantees that we'll produce best-selling work. As that great philosopher and Stanley Cup winner Wayne Gretzky once said, "You miss one hundred percent of the shots you don't take." Yes, if you don't try, you will fail. It's guaranteed.

Writers work through the fears. It's a tough truth, but something you'll need to face.

Writers don't buy into these myths told and accepted by civilians (remember, that's what I call nonwriters). Writing is work. But once you've been bitten by the writing bug, there is no other journey on which you'd rather be.

Can You Make It as a Writer?

Can you make it as a writer? This is a huge question and one you may have been wrestling with for some time, maybe even years. It could be that your spouse, kids, parents, and co-workers are longing to ask the question but haven't—*yet*. Or have they?

The truth is that anyone with tenacity and a measure of creativity can become a good writer and a published writer. If you are a survivor, an overachiever, and a worrywart, you'll be even more likely to be successful. (That's advice from your fellow surviving, overachieving, worrying mentor.)

How can you make your career "happen"? If you weren't born into a family that owns a huge publishing conglomerate, then you do the work and hone your craft. You become a wordsmith. How much work? Whatever it takes. But first answer this question: Are you happy, exhilarated, challenged, and determined when writing? If you answered yes, then you would be crazy to give up something that makes you feel this way.

Today, sharing your work with other writers in a critique group is considered cool. If that's true, I'm not cool, and I'd like you to consider being uncool with me. Sharing work too soon can destroy the creative process. I can better use the time I would spend in a group by actually doing what I do best—writing. This is especially true if, like me, you have family, other work or volunteer commitments, home, church, and a host of responsibilities.

Instead, learn the craft. Study it like your future depends on it, because if your future includes writing for publication, then it does. Take classes (online, on campus, and at conferences), and attend book-related events.

If you have negative people in your life, or perhaps you've started to write before but became detoured, simply don't mention what you're doing. Okay, tell your spouse or partner, but keep the writing to yourself until you're ready. You'll know when.

Ignore anyone who says, "You've got to be born with it." Prove 'em wrong. With practice, you'll improve.

I have played golf and tennis, and Joe (my husband) and I recently took ballroom dance classes. The superstars in these activities/sports never, ever, ever have to worry about me being a serious competitor. Yes, Tiger Woods, you are safe.

Seriously, just because I won't be on *Dancing with the Stars* or asked to compete at Wimbledon doesn't mean I can't enjoy the activity. I love writing limericks, and I am not going to stop even though many think limericks are the McDonald's fast food of poetry.

What does all this mean to you, because this book is most definitely about you? It means that if you enjoy writing, write for the joy of it. Treat it like it's a worthy endeavor, and put in the time you need to get better at it.

Here's a plan.

1. Write every day, in this book. Do it during lunch break or while waiting for the kids.

2. Read books by writers on writing.

3. Give yourself time to evolve. Odds are, you crawled before you walked and definitely walked before you ran.

Now here's the final part. Look in the mirror. Smile. That's a writer facing you. Can you see it in the eyes? Could you tell this person that writing is all a bunch of foolishness? Not if you're honest.

Really now, what alternative do you have? If you have the heart to write, you must.

What Writers Really Need

As a writer, what are your basic needs? Why not make a list?

I bet they're pretty much like the list of things that most of us strive for. What is it that writers need that civilians don't? I believe we need a thirsty curiosity and a bundle of tenacity. As we talked about, a wall covered with degrees, a trust fund, and unlimited time to write don't seem to make a difference in the success (personal and publishable) of a writer, but rather it's that wanting-to-know part of our minds that makes us writers.

After the necessities of life (that is, water, food, shelter, and a debt-free credit card), writers need a quiet place to work. Oh, yes, I know of a colleague who always writes in the evening (he's a chiropractor by day) in the family room with five kids, two dogs, and a spouse all watching television, doing homework, playing board games, and talking on the phone. I would go nuts. There are always exceptions to the rules, but I believe a quiet room or spot to write is essential.

Now, your quiet spot might be a table at the library or an overstuffed chair at the local java joint. Seek out your spot, and like we did when we were kids, put dibs on it.

At home find a spot, nook, or cranny where you can sit quietly, maybe in the garden or on the porch, even better. When I first started writing, I worked on a typewriter (yes, it was back in the Bronze Age) at the dining room table. It was actually a rented typewriter because I wanted to make sure I had what it took to be a writer before I bought all that fancy computer equipment—which I coveted, I might add.

Once the family left for the day, I brought out my typewriter, found a cushion so that I could be comfortable on a stiff chair, and wrote. I wrote how-to articles. I wrote for confession magazines. I wrote short stories and poems. And I sent them off to magazines, just like it said to do in *Writer's Market*.

Sound idyllic? It was quiet until about three in the afternoon when our youngest (who was a child at the time) dashed in from school with news of his day, typically with starving buddies in tow. Four o'clock came tumbling at me, and I knew I had to close up shop. I needed to get dinner together. My husband would be hungry when he came through the door (and I was usually starving by this time anyhow), and I didn't want to (1) have the family eat over the freshly typed manuscripts, and (2) share my work with anyone. I did this for about a year and then realized it was time, as Virginia Woolf tells us, to have a room of my own.

It was scary for me, but I had to do it if I was going to be a real writer. I cleaned the family out of the family room. I moved the television to the living room. I bought some secondhand furniture, and I designated the former family room as my office. I practiced saying things like, "If you need me, I'll be in my office," and "I'm going to be in my office writing so please keep the TV down," and "When the coffee is brewed, I'd love a cup in my office." Okay, it sounds silly, but I wanted to convince myself that writing was my business. Every businessperson has an office.

There is something in us writers that yearns for that room, that sanctuary for aloneness. If you're craving it, please do what you can to make it happen. No, you may not have the luxury of that extra bedroom or den or even a family that can be exiled from your work space. The best is to be creative. Stay an hour after work when everyone leaves and write. Come in early. See if you can use the computer at the office on Saturday afternoon. Is there a tiny spot in the kitchen where you can set up the computer and leave your work in progress? Grab it. If it's an unused corner of the garage or a forgotten playhouse in the garden, snag it. You will upgrade later.

The Must-Know Tool: The Bubble Method

The Bubble Method, sometimes called clustering and mind mapping, is a brainstorming technique used by fiction and nonfiction writers. It's a powerful creative tool if you want to discover the unexpected and to clarify thoughts.

The method works whether you're brainstorming for a query letter, interview questions, article topics, or to come up with ideas that you're interested in writing books about. (For your information: The Bubble Method also works well to develop plots and characterization if you're also a fiction writer.) The Bubble Method is a winner if you want to brainstorm titles, too, and it's great when you're trying to come up with names for characters in your fiction work.

Using this method for writing articles makes writing them so simple that if you "subbubble," that is, take each subtopic and use the Bubble Method again, the article will write itself.

If there's one bit of information I'll keep my fingers crossed that you'll use, it's the Bubble Method. People in my traditional and online classes and during my writer's conference workshops gush at length about the concept, and yet it's simple.

Here are the directions to bubble for an article idea. If you're brainstorming for a book, a chapter, or another creative endeavor, just substitute the focus:

Get a large piece of newsprint paper and crayons or colored marking pens. You may not use typing/printer paper and writing pens. You need to THINK BIG.

Print the topic of your article in the middle of a piece of paper. Draw a circle around the words. Add ten lines straight out from the circle, or the first bubble. You have made what looks like a child's drawing of the sun with words in the center.

Without censoring yourself in any way (seriously, shut your fears or reservations outside of your house when doing the Bubble Method), print ten subtopics that are somehow related to your main topic. Circle them, too. That's it. Simple and powerful.

Do not stop with seven or nine. You must brainstorm until you have ten or more topics on that paper. Why ten? Because the first six or seven topics or ideas or characteristics are easy, but I have found when I get to the ninth or tenth item, my creativity kicks into overtime. It is then that good ideas really flow.

Sit back and look at the fresh ideas the system produced. Read the ideas out loud.

After you have reviewed your second bubbles, select those that seem to be sufficient to support an entire article. (A small, simple topic might not be sufficient to propose for a two-thousand-word article. It might be better in a two-hundred-word article.) Try to come up with seven to nine. If you cannot comfortably include seven, return to step 1 or consider doing some more research to learn about your proposed topic. Choose your favorite for the next assignment.

Take each of the sub-bubbles individually and bubble again. With this go-round you're actually outlining your article and will come up with seven to ten topics. These are the main points of your article; perhaps they're the topics of the article's paragraphs. You may want to bubble down further and outline sub-sub-bubbles.

After you have bubbled and like the focus of the article, put the entire thing away for a day or so if you can. Try not to consciously think about the bubbles during this time, and I promise your brain will be silently mulling up massive loads of creativity.

After a day or two and without looking at the previous bubbles, go back and repeat the entire method. Finally, compare the two. Then put the material in list form. You'll have a map to take you to the completion of your article, essay, nonfiction book, story, or novel.

The system is easy and addictive. I use it often and use it when I write articles and books, create book proposals, and help students discover the writing fields in which they want to focus. You'll want to use the Bubble Method, found here in the information section of the book, to help brainstorm ideas.

Why *Do* Books Fail?

A few years ago, I taught a six-week course for writers at the University of California, Riverside. I love teaching in person as well as online. That session my students nudged me (what I call a gentle nudge) to tell them why books failed to be accepted by agents and/or publishers. I didn't want to. I wanted them to think that they were invincible and that with time, practice, and tenacity they'd get published. After four weeks, a group caught up with me as I was leaving the campus. Not quite a mob, but they were serious.

"It's okay if you don't want to tell the others," said the ringleader, a lady in her sixties who was writing a memoir. "But we've talked, and we must know why books fail."

So that they'd let me get into my SUV, I promised to lecture on the topic at the next session. Here's a version of what I told those writers.

Every year in the United States, more than 250,000 new books are presented to readers. Only a few make it to best-seller lists. Most fail.

The majority of these books that do not make it to the bookstore, best-seller lists, or back for a second printing fail to do so for seven reasons.

- Confusion. Are you clear on the genre, the point of view, the thesis? Books have categories, or genres, and too often emerging authors do not study the genre that they're targeting, or they change genres while writing. This doesn't mean one needs to be a copycat; rather, by reading in the genre to be targeted, one becomes familiar with length, structure, and concept. Go to a brick-and-mortar bookstore and find the section where your book would be. Check the competition. What do they have you don't? And vice versa? What added value does your book provide? Memorize these facts. You'll need them to sell your book.

- Lack of original insight. It's been said, "There's nothing new under the sun." However, smart authors create twists to make the "old stuff" fresh. What's your twist? Don't know? Find out, get help, talk to others who know about originality and marketing.

- Poor or ineffective research. If you're in doubt about the authenticity of anything in your book, whether it's fiction or nonfiction, double-check. Readers demand truth; the public is leery of unsubstantiated claims.

- Insufficient self-editing. You really can do most of the polishing yourself. Put your book away to cool. Then, keeping a copy, ruthlessly edit out anything that doesn't strongly support your book. Hint: Look for redundancy or repetition. Readers don't need to be told things twice. That last sentence was an example of sneaky redundancy. If you're not a native English speaker or want some insight, hire a reputable content or copy editor.

- Hook-less beginning (for each chapter or section) or lackluster end. Readers are fair and will give you about ten minutes' time reading your book to prove that they should spend money on it. However, everything in the book—especially the chapter beginnings—must hook the reader. This takes skill with nonfiction and fiction. The end must fulfill the promises you've proposed in the text and support your thesis. It must be done in a creative, fresh way.

- Bad mechanics. If you need to brush up on grammar or the mechanics of manuscript preparation, do it before sending out review copies. Hire a professional even if you have a degree in English from Harvard. After reading a manuscript twice or twenty times, the eye skips over mistakes. As a much-published writer and ghost, I admit to typo and grammar blindness. It's an embarrassing condition once the book is published. Don't let it happen to you.

- Lack of perseverance. Publishing and writing are not for wimps. The hard work starts when the boxes of books arrive. Hire a PR pro, or do it yourself. How? Write articles based on the premise of your nonfiction book to get exposure, lure book buyers, and generate income. For fiction, create "events" by teaching hopeful writers about the technical side of your genre. A signing shouts you're selling the book (which is true), but an event is an activity. Then the attendee buys your book. Get that elevator speech down: explain your book in twenty-five words or fewer, and get comfy whipping business cards out and extending your hand. Ask for business; ask people to buy your book. The worst that can happen? If you're going to stop being a publisher or a writer when you hear the word "no," move on over. There are hundreds of others who want to take your place. I call this "literary Darwinism," and I'll be first in line to take your place.

Best Sellers with Big Rejection Records

The list of best-selling books that were rejected again and again is shocking. Here is a baker's dozen:

1. *Dubliners* by James Joyce

2. *Mash* by Richard Hooker

3. *Heaven Knows, Mr. Allison* by Charles Shaw

4. *Kon-Tiki* by Thor Heyerdahl

5. *Jonathan Livingston Seagull* by Richard Bach

6. *The Postman Always Rings Twice* by James M. Cain

7. *Chicken Soup for the Soul* books by Hansen, Canfield

8. *Auntie Mame* by Patrick Dennis

9. *The Peter Principle* by Laurence Peter

10. *Dune* by Frank Herbert

11. *Harry Potter* series by J. K. Rowling

12. *Peter Rabbit* series by Beatrix Potter

13. *60-Second Shiatzu* by Eva Shaw

More on Rejection

My first book, *60-Second Shiatzu*, was rejected by forty-nine publishers, but since that time, it's been reprinted nine times in the United States and throughout the United Kingdom with Simon and Schuster; lots of magazines have picked up excerpts, and thirteen foreign publishers have published it. This has happened to many authors and on many books. My story isn't special, but unless you can face disappointment that may or may not come and keep writing, then you cannot be a freelancer.

Decide today, or at least by next week, how a few rejections are going to affect you. If you quit with just a few, or more than forty, will you ever really know if you have what it takes?

Hey, Just Look at Self-Editing

Some writers write to untangle feelings and thoughts. They might journal or blog. Some write to gain self-esteem, to realize a dream. In a recent poll published in *USA Today*, surveyors found that 80 percent of adults had a book inside them that they wanted to come out.

A writer can't be a writer without producing words, so some people merely dream. On the other hand, not all of us are seeking publication. Not all of us want to pen the Great American Novel or the next *New York Times* nonfiction best seller. But some of us do.

Regardless of your goals for writing, self-editing is as important as the writing process. I do about ten drafts of my work. Some are on the screen, some on paper. I usually read one of those drafts aloud because I find that if I trip over the words, my readers surely will.

It's my opinion, as the author of more than seventy books and having worked with thousands of emerging writers, self-editing is the biggest need and the biggest challenge. It's what many think that they can skip over rather than putting in the time to polish their writing. Okay, I agree. Self-editing isn't one of the fun jobs in writing, but it is necessary.

I highly urge you not to edit your writing until it's finished. Spill out the ideas and words, let them pour forth, and then, after you've let the manuscript cool for at least twenty-four hours (or more), go back and edit.

A few years ago in a traditional writing class on a university campus, Nikki had a really hard time with this concept. A bright woman of about twenty, she was determined to be a published novelist. She told the class and me, "Every word I put down is there for a reason, and it couldn't and shouldn't be changed." It all sounds very mystical and nice, but her stream-of-consciousness writing was just that: rambling. That's fine and dandy if Nikki was a celebrity or a high-profile politician or had already made a name for herself in publishing, but that wasn't the case.

Here are some tips:

With dialogue, every character gets his or her own tag line. A tag line is the "said" part of dialogue, as in: "I've smashed smaller ones in the garden. You will not ever see me eat snails no matter what swanky name you call them," said Aunt Matilda to the French waiter.

A big problem with many writers I have coached is redundancy, the sneaky kind where one says things twice, almost so, as in: "Humpty Dumpty decided to run for governor. He was a good egg all around, but as a governor he'd have to be hard-boiled since candidates really needed a sturdy shell."

OK, that's pretty silly, but in the case of our good-egg governor, hard shell and hard-boiled have a redundancy that makes reading boring.

Watch, too, for changes in verb tense. If you choose present tense (I run everyday), stick with it throughout the story or article.

Consider word choices and sentence structure as you are self-editing. If you're showing and not telling in a story or book, you can influence the feelings of the reader through language. That's a fancy way of telling you to make the words reflect the storyline. Here's an example: Run. Run. Footsteps. He's after me. No, not again.

Here, the short jolts of energy give the reader a feeling that the protagonist is moving quickly, somewhat fearfully.

What if it was written: There is someone running after her, and she can hear the footsteps. He is there again.

OK, we'll know that someone is after the protagonist, but we can't feel the intensity of the chase.

In nonfiction, the use of the question is a powerful tool because it's interactive with the reader. Often, we use questions as hooks for our reader.

- Do you know what your cat does when you're away?

- How safe is your drinking water?

- Should the government quit minting pennies?

- Have you cheated on your hairdresser?

As you become Sherlock Holmes or Miss Marple and really investigate your genre, as we've discussed before, you'll see how those who have been published create dialogue, moods, and feelings. What verb tense do they use? Why? How are characters developed, and how do they speak? This information is readily available to help guide you as you self-edit your work.

Before you break the rules of grammar and forget the need to polish your prose, learn what you need. *Self-Editing for Fiction Writers* by Browne and King is a book on this topic, and it's great for both fiction and nonfiction writers. The authors stress the mechanics of writing from point of view (POV) to writing interior dialogue.

Your Writeriffic Writing Assignments

Here are your creativity assignments. I promise you, they will increase your skill as a creative writer, but only if you do them. As my mama said, "Talk is cheap." If you have only talked about writing up to now, stop that talk and start to write.

Some of the assignments have variations, so there are really enough of them to last a year. You might want to write on extra paper and then copy your writing onto the pages following each exercise in this journal. I hope you'll write directly into this book so you can see how your voice gains power and evolves.

The extra pages at the back of this book are for your creative variations on the assignments. Don't write as if you're attempting to please your high school English teacher or even Great Aunt Gertrude. He or she will never see this creative work, so you're safe. Further, the Grammar and Spelling Police do not walk this beat. Have fun. Take risks. Just create.

When you have done all the assignments, heard your writer's voice, and felt your creative energies surging, contact me. I want to hear about the hurdles that you've climbed over and the successes you've had. I want to know what works for you and what doesn't. I want to know about other creativity assignments you've used. I want to be your mentor.

Choosing Words: Creating a Story

Open a dictionary and select a word that you're not familiar with. Write it down. Repeat this until you've collected ten new-to-you words. Then, using these ten words, create a story of 1,000 words using one or more of the following as your protagonist.

- Robin Hood
- Marilyn Monroe
- Cinderella
- Dorothy from *The Wizard of Oz*
- Arthur "The Fonz" Fonzerelli from *Happy Days*
- Hannah Montana
- James Dean
- Eleanor Roosevelt
- Abraham Lincoln
- Cleopatra
- Scarlet O'Hara
- John Lennon
- Olive Oyl
- Henry David Thoreau
- Beatrix Potter
- Hester Prynne
- George W. Patton

- Minnie Mouse
- Count Dracula
- C. S. Lewis
- Joan of Arc
- Dorothy Parker
- Sherlock Holmes
- Martin Luther King, Jr.
- Mother Teresa
- Mary Worth
- Pillsbury Doughboy
- Robert the Bruce
- Peter Parker (who is *Spider-Man*)
- Johnny Appleseed
- Florence Nightingale
- Big Bird from *Sesame Street*
- Betsy Ross
- Harry Potter
- Albert Schweitzer

Date _____ Title _____

_____

_____

_____

_____

_____

_____

_____

_____

_____

_____

_____

_____

_____

_____

_____

_____

_____

_____

_____

_____

_____

_____

_____

_____

_____

_____

_____

_____

_____

_____

_____

_____ _____ *Continued on page* _____

Feed Your Creative Self

Go online or remember the recipe for a favorite childhood food. My mama always made gingerbread cookies at Christmas, heavy on the nutmeg, and I can "taste" them in my mind when I think of this holiday.

OR: cook something that is a favorite, and before you begin to indulge, smell, feel, taste on your tongue, and capture these senses in your writing.

Once you've focused on the memories and flavors in your mind, write 200 words on this memory.

For overachievers: Write this using only dialogue and appropriate tag lines (the he-said, she-said attributions).

Date _____   Title _____

_____

_____

_____

_____

_____

_____

_____

_____

_____

_____

_____

_____

_____

Continued on page _____

Rewrite an Article

Pick up a copy of your favorite magazine or newsletter, whether it's *Glamour* or *Organic Gardening*, *Dairy Farming News* or *Concrete Construction Report*. Select one article. Identify the hook, normally the first sentence or two. Rewrite the article, turning it into a short story or an essay, but *you must use the same hook*.

Keep your word count to about 1,000 words.

Date _____ Title _____

_____

_____

_____

_____

_____

_____

_____

_____

_____

_____

_____

_____

_____

_____

_____

_____

_____

Continued on page _____

Change That Name

Using the Bubble Method, choose the protagonist from your favorite novel, and change his/her/its name. Will Peter Pan be changed to Timothy Tuttle? Will Jane Eyre become Jessica Lee? Could Harry Potter become Chris Light Feather? Then, using the form below, create a brand-new character. If you decide you like this character, feature him/her/it in a new story of no more than 1,000 words.

The Character Sketch Form

Name: _____

Nickname: _____

Appearance—Hair: _____ Eyes: _____ Mouth: _____ Nose: _____

Weight: _____ Height: _____ Build: _____ Hands: _____

Voice accent/way of talking: _____

Birthday: _____

Family members: _____

Siblings/best friends: _____

Ethnic/cultural background: _____

Schooling: _____

Occupation: _____

Hobbies: _____

Addictions: _____

Political preference: _____

Religious preference: _____

Nightmares: _____

Favorite movie/book: _____

Favorite foods: _____

Favorite sports: _____

Fears/phobias: _____

Quirks and character flaws: _____

Favorite expression: _____

Worst teen memory: _____

Role model: _____

Date _____ Title _____

Continued on page _____

Quote It

After reading one of the following quotes, write an essay and use the quote for the first line. Consider submitting the essay to a site, magazine or local newspaper after you've reviewed the publications' guidelines.

- Madame de Stael: The mystery of existence is the connection between our faults and our misfortunes.

- Will Rogers: Half our life is spent trying to find something to do with the time we have rushed through life trying to save.

- Dorothy Thompson: Only when we are no longer afraid do we begin to live.

- Zig Ziglar: You can get everything in life you want if you will just help enough other people get what they want.

- Unknown: Life would be much easier if I had the source code.

- Mark Twain: Twenty years from now you will be more disappointed by the things you didn't do than by the ones you did do. So throw off the bowlines. Sail away from the safe harbor. Catch the trade winds in your sails. Explore. Dream. Discover.

- Robert Frost: What is this talked-of mystery of birth but being mounted bareback on the earth?

- Anais Nin: People living deeply have no fear of death.

Date _____ Title _____

_____

_____

_____

_____

_____

_____

_____

_____

_____

_____

_____

_____

_____

_____

_____

_____

_____

_____

_____

_____

_____

_____

_____

_____

_____

_____

_____

_____

_____

_____

_____

_____

_____   *Continued on page* _____

If Romeo and Juliet Had Lived

Okay, we all know what happened to these star-crossed lovers, but what might happen if they lived in this decade and had to cope with cultural and economic factors, ethnic distrust and hatred, with one family pitted against the other? Select one of the large cities in your state, select the lovers' backgrounds, and then identify why the families are at war. It might be because one is disabled or disfigured. It could be that the families have always looked down on a certain ethnic group. The story focus could even be between alien races.

Retell Shakespeare's classic, in an outline form or a story of no more than 500-750 words. Use plenty of dialogue. Don't remember the story? You can read the play online by popping *Romeo and Juliet* in on www.Google.com.

For overachievers: Use a variation of Juliet's famous balcony scene in your story:

> O Romeo, Romeo,
>
> wherefore art thou Romeo?
>
> Deny thy father and refuse thy name,
>
> Or if thou wilt not, be but sworn my love,
>
> And I'll no longer be a Capulet.

Date _____   Title _____

_____

_____

_____

_____

_____

Continued on page _____

Limerick—Be a Poet and Know It

Create an original limerick on any subject you like.

A limerick is a short, comical, and almost musical poem that often borders on the nonsensical or obscene, such as:

There was a young lady one fall

Who wore a newspaper dress to a ball.

The dress caught fire

And burned her entire

Front page, sporting section, and all.

WikiHow.com and other Web sites will teach you how to create one. You can find rhyming words by doing a search online, or your public library should have a rhyming dictionary.

For your information, the limerick was popularized in England by Edward Lear (Limerick Day is celebrated on his birthday, May 12). Writing them takes a little practice at first, but before long you'll be addicted to coming up with these witty, whimsical rhymes. The following is by Edward Lear:

There was an Old Person whose habits,

Induced him to feed upon rabbits;

When he'd eaten eighteen,

He turned perfectly green,

Upon which he relinquished those habits.

Date _____ Title _____

_____

_____

_____

_____

_____

_____

_____

_____

_____

_____

_____

_____

_____

_____

_____

_____

_____

_____

_____

_____

_____

_____

_____

_____

_____

_____

_____

Continued on page _____

Write a Banned-Book Review

Banned Books Week (BBW) celebrates our freedom to read. It is observed during the last week of September each year.

Observed since 1982, this annual American Library Association event reminds Americans not to take this precious democratic freedom for granted. Check www.ala.org for the dates of this year's BBW.

According to the America Library Association, "BBW celebrates the freedom to choose or the freedom to express one's opinion even if that opinion might be considered unorthodox or unpopular and stresses the importance of ensuring the availability of those unorthodox or unpopular viewpoints to all who wish to read them. After all, intellectual freedom can exist only where these two essential conditions are met."

Do an online search for titles of some (surprising) banned books, such as *Grapes of Wrath, Tom Sawyer, A Wrinkle in Time, Call of the Wild,* and *To Kill a Mockingbird.* Read summaries about the books. Read book reviews that you can find in newspapers and magazines so that you become familiar with the style.

Now write a pro or con review of one of the books to support your opinion that it should be kept or dismissed from the list. You may need to read the book or review it from info you can find at the library or on Amazon.com. About three months prior to BBW, consider submitting your review to a newspaper or other publication that accepts freelance submissions.

Date _____   Title _____

_____

_____

_____

_____

_____

Continued on page _____

Age Related

Write the numbers 5, 10, 15, 18, 21, 35, 50 on this workbook's lined pages or on separate pieces of paper.

Now, before picking up a pen, think about who you were at these ages or who you will be.

Describe yourself then, now, or in the future, as you might with a character in a novel.

Write no more than 100 words. Avoid giving height, weight, color of eyes or hair. Be descriptive and write as if you are telling about a character.

Now, for a "big" birthday year, what goals did you have? How do they reflect on who you are today?

Possibilities: Write about the music, food, clothing, slang, styles, hobbies, family, parties, high school, or friends who affected you.

Look within yourself for the feelings and motivators you use in fictional characters.

Use the extra pages in the back of the journal to write about other milestone birthdays or events in your life.

Date _____ Title _____

_____

_____

_____

_____

_____

_____

Continued on page _____

Write a Letter

Write a letter or e-mail to your favorite author. If the person is alive, track down an address and send it to her/him.

In your letter explain what his/her writing means or meant to you, and be specific. Depending on your memory and/or if you want to quote passages, you might need to revisit the book you're writing about.

Date _____   Title _____

_____

_____

_____

_____

_____

_____

_____

_____

_____

_____

_____

_____

_____

_____

_____

_____

Continued on page _____

Reading for Fun

Because what we read for fun is typically the genre we know the best and often the best genre for our writing, write a list of your favorite books, followed by the genre.

Now, in 200 words or fewer, write a book review of your favorite contemporary book.

If you want to, find a home for the review on Amazon.com or another of the book-buying sites.

Date _____ Title _____

_____

_____

_____

_____

_____

_____

_____

_____

_____

_____

_____

_____

_____

_____

_____

_____

_____

_____

Continued on page _____

Change the Hook

Pick up a copy of your favorite magazine, or go to your favorite magazine's online version. Your local library probably has magazines that you may never have read.

Select an article, review its hook (the sentence or two that pulls you into the magazine's article), and pretend you're the editor of a magazine. You must—before the next editorial meeting that is (gasp!) in twenty minutes—create *ten* different hooks.

For instance, let's say the hook for a food article is this: Cucumbers are fun. You know that won't make readers read this article, so you brainstorm others such as:

Cucumbers are a foodie beauty secret.

What germs cling to cucumber skin?

Pesticides can cancel cucumbers health benefits.

Cucumber-flavored baby food?

Does anyone eat cucumber sandwiches?

Relish homemade cucumber relish.

Green gold—nutritional clout of cucumbers.

Let this cool, and then play with the hooks. This is a fun game to do when you're waiting for an appointment and only have a stack of magazines to keep your writing brain satisfied.

Date _____ Title _____

_____

_____

_____

_____

_____

_____

_____

_____

_____

_____

_____

_____

_____

_____

_____

_____

_____

_____

_____

_____

_____

_____

_____

_____

_____

_____

_____

_____

_____ *Continued on page* _____

Finish the Story

Select one of the phrases below, and fill the next page with your story. Be creative. Want an extra challenge? Use dialogue or develop a twist for the ending

- The first shovelful was tough, but then ...

- My sister made me crazy when she ...

- Tuna and sauerkraut fritters? Stanley's cooking became ...

- "Morty's at it again," she gulped and ...

- We called it "the incident" after Lee ...

- White shoes after Labor Day was nothing compared to ...

- "Darling, no one will find out," CJ assured ...

- Some stains come out, but blood ...

- Pat and Jay counted the $100 bills. Then they heard ...

- It was no use. Joan could never ...

- As everyone left the office, Jinx pulled out a file on ...

- Loading the truck was easy. Hiding the contents got messy because ...

- Snow fell like a ...

- Gasoline, rags, and $2 million. Let me tell my side of what happened ...

- The room fell silent as Georgie ...

Ponder ideas before you begin writing. With so many stories to finish and so many genres to choose from, you can do a variation of this exercise every day for a month.

Date _____ Title _____

_____

_____

_____

_____

_____

_____

_____

_____

_____

_____

_____

_____

_____

_____

_____

_____

_____

_____

_____

_____

_____

_____

_____

_____

_____

_____

_____

_____

_____

_____ *Continued on page* _____

Don't Get Arrested

Eavesdrop. Yes, listen up. Inspiration from snatches of conversation are everywhere. Find a very public place, and listen to the conversations. I love to do this at fast-food restaurants, libraries, and cafés. Starbucks was made for this assignment, and the commuter bus or the office's lunchroom are excellent choices. It might help to pretend you're reading.

Take along a pad and pencil and, as you eat, watch other people. Make notes of facial features, laughs, body movements. You need to know how people talk, walk, and eat so that you can put this information into your writing. Don't stalk people. You could be arrested.

Be on the lookout for one person who begs to be part of a short story. Kids, teens, and seniors are often the best people to observe because they're less cautious with their behavior.

Ask yourself "what if?" What if the teenager is a math wizard or a real wizard, like Harry Potter? What if that grandmother is a secret agent like Dorothy Gilman's Mrs. Polifax? What if that busy mom will win the Lotto or is an alien from another galaxy?

Write enough to fill up this and the following page.

Date _____ Title _____

_____

_____

_____

_____

_____

_____

Continued on page _____

Make a Prose Sandwich

Part 1: Write about your favorite way to make a sandwich. This is fun to do in poetry, too.

Part 2: Write at least 200 words on why you like the sandwich.

Part 3: Create a story making the sandwich a focal point.

Need some ideas? You can start with these and then create your own.

Does the protagonist (your main character) get the kids to eat vegetables by stuffing pita with zucchini?

Will the villain take one bite and turn into Miss Goody Two-Shoes?

Why did the ruthless tycoon finance a sandwich boutique owned by a penniless grandmother?

Date _____ Title _____

_____

_____

_____

_____

_____

_____

_____

_____

_____

_____

Continued on page _____

He Said, She Said

Using only dialogue and tag lines (the attribution that usually includes the word *said*), write a short story of no more than 200 to 500 words.

Include location, two or three characters, an event (birth of a child, being fired, getting married, passing a test), and think of a twist for the end. Humor works, so you might want to research jokes and see if you can include a joke as the twist at the end.

Here's what one story might look like:

"Don't point that thing at me, young lady. No daughter of mine packs a pistol."

"Mother, it's a water pistol. Don't you want to be cool? You're always saying that Dad's cool, so now you can be, too. Besides tomorrow's your fiftieth birthday, Mom. You're only going to be forty-nine for ten more hours. When you're fifty, you aren't a kid anymore; at least, that's what Aunt Margaret said."

"I don't give a flying pig about being cool, being a kid, or your confounded Aunt Margaret, Susie. I've seen guns like that on TV. It's a Super Slosher."

"I got it from a 'But Wait!' commercial. I bought two for the same price. I was going to give it to you wrapped, but this is better."

"Hand that thing over. Oops, sorry, honey, I didn't know this thing was loaded."

Never once were you told that this is a conversation between parent and child, but that quickly came out in the dialogue. Make that your goal.

Date _____ Title _____

_____
_____
_____
_____
_____
_____
_____
_____
_____

_____
_____
_____
_____
_____
_____
_____
_____
_____
_____
_____

_____ *Continued on page* _____

Wallet Writing

Take out your wallet, and put three objects you've found inside on the table in front of you. These might be your Costco card, driver's license, or even money. It will be a more creative challenge if you don't use photos of the family or your pets. Instead, choose items you rarely think about.

Study the objects for at least five minutes. If appropriate, you might want to carry the objects in your pocket for the next few hours or even sleep with them beneath your pillow. Sound odd? All creativity is innovative and, if these ideas feel right, then they are.

It's a requirement that you sit quietly and touch, smell, feel, and study the objects for at least five minutes. If necessary, set an alarm so you don't budge until the time's up.

Your goal is to tell the story of why each is important to you. Is there a story connected to it? Do you, for example, remember how you quivered with excitement to get your driver's license? Or cringed when the AARP card came in the mail?

Write at least 200 words about these objects. Write this in essay form, that is, in first person. Reveal something about yourself that you may never have told any other person.

Remember, as with other assignments, you do not need to share this.

Date _____ Title _____

_____

_____

_____

_____

_____

Continued on page _____

Yes, I Did Learn It Myself

What did you learn? What did you teach yourself? Write 400 words or more about whatever you've learned and why it has been valuable.

Some of the experiences I've had in life could be considered negative, but I've learned from them. Negative experiences and negative people can be our best teachers.

You can write about learning to tie your shoes, drive a car with a manual transmission, create software, or craft a soft blanket.

If you need a nudge (my gentle way of pushing), explain why you learned a tough lesson, your loves and hates at the time, what was happening in your world, and how you felt or feel about the lesson.

Date _____ Title _____

_____

_____

_____

_____

_____

_____

_____

_____

_____

_____

Continued on page _____

Dive into Nature

Go outside. Sit and find something that is in nature.

Write for five minutes or until you fill these pages on some aspect of nature—perhaps a cloud, maybe the wind, or even a fallen leaf.

Write poetry, write fragmented sentences, or draw a sketch in this journal. There are so many variations on this exercise that you could spend a year or more writing about nature. Longfellow, Thoreau, and Muir all did.

Can't get outside? Go online to one of the national botanical gardens, and write about what you're seeing on the screen.

Note for overachievers: This is an excellent assignment to warm up your creative writing muscles. Why not start every writing session with a variation of the above?

Date _____   Title _____

_____

_____

_____

_____

_____

_____

_____

_____

_____

_____

_____

Continued on page _____

Play with Words

Take out your dictionary, and open it anywhere.

Let your finger move up and down the page, with or without looking at where it's moving. Stop at any time.

Take this word and learn its meaning. Then use it as the focal point of a short story. It's better if you're not truly familiar with the word—that is, it's more challenging and fun.

For instance, the word I've selected is "twaddle." Here's the beginning of a story:

"Twaddle," I mumbled back at the woman's statement that I had to finish my pureed carrots.

"Say that again, missy, and you're in big trouble," growled the babysitter.

"Twaddle!" I screamed. "Your theories on nutrition are absolute twaddle." If not for the walker, I could have gotten away from that woman my kids hired to look after me while they were at work.

Oh, the possibilities of what could happen next. Now it's your turn. If you enjoy this exercise, you might want to use it to start out every writing session. The possibilities are unlimited.

Date _____ Title _____

_____

_____

_____

_____

Continued on page _____

Picture This

Take a picture out of your family photo album. Find one in which you are prominent and, preferably, one of you as a child or younger.

Are you standing with a sibling or family member? Maybe it's a class photo where all the kids look bright and scrubbed.

Perhaps you've taken a picture from a birthday party. There you are with your grandparents hovering in the background. Maybe you're a teenager and posed against your new car, a banged-up Ford that you thought was hot stuff.

Study the photo for about five minutes. Set the timer if you think you'll have trouble with this part of the exercise. Use the photograph as a vehicle to time travel back to the memory of that exact day.

Here's what to look for:

- Background—Grass, dirt, house, a city street.

- Facial expressions—Upset, happy, faking a smile, naïve, frustrated, silly.

- Clothing—Casual, torn, mismatched, party clothes.

- Season—Just before the first day of school, stuffed into a hand-me-down snowsuit.

- Location—Kitchen table, Yosemite National Park, Aunt Millie's fishing pond.

- Accessories—Toys, dolls, sporting equipment.

- Details—Bandages on a skinned knee, a terrible haircut, the cat curling around your ankles, the dog pulling on your swimsuit.

Make some notes on paper or on the computer. Continue to look at the picture. Feel the moment.

Trust me; you'll remember everything once you stare hard enough at the photograph. Don't be surprised if you once again feel anger, hurt, or bliss. These are some of the emotions you'll want to use when you're writing your life story or creating characters for that novel.

You may even want to clear your mind and close your eyes for a few moments before you begin. It helps to relax and maybe meditate so you can relive some of the emotions you experienced at that time in your life. Make some more notes about how you will write the photo essay, but don't start yet.

Need ideas? You can tell about the day, what happened, what didn't happen, why you were there, or how it feels to see yourself as a child.

Although I don't remember the day, because I was just two at the time, one of my favorite pictures is of my sisters and me. We're lined up on a shabby sofa that had been covered with a granny-square afghan. My grandmother Paulina crocheted it during the Great Depression. Because my grandmother couldn't afford new yarn, the afghan was made by unraveling cast-off sweaters, a practice that today seems as foreign as traveling in covered wagons.

Because I've memorized the stories behind the photographs in our family album, I know this one was taken the day before we left New Jersey, just after my younger sister was born. I look at those three little girls and marvel at my parents' bravery, or foolishness, to trek along old Route 66 to California with three tiny kids, one of whom was just days old.

Then, in my mind's eye, I see the three of us as adults and wonder what life might have been like if we had grown up along the shore in New Jersey, near overprotective grandparents and the traditions that had stifled my parents. I feel sorrow because a few years ago my younger sister lost her battle with cancer. I feel joy to be close to my older sister although we're separated by hundreds of miles. And I'm nearly teary-eyed looking at that afghan that now has an honored place in my own living room.

Those are my feelings and thoughts based on a photo.

Now write yours. Use the following page. Here again, you might want to jot down some ideas or ponder the assignment before you begin.

This assignment has many variations, and the possibilities are only limited by your supply of old photos.

Date _____ Title _____

_____
_____
_____
_____
_____
_____
_____
_____
_____
_____
_____
_____
_____
_____
_____
_____
_____
_____
_____
_____
_____
_____
_____
_____
_____
_____ *Continued on page* _____

Alien Animal Power

Go online to one of the Web sites for a national zoo or the San Diego Wild Animal Park.

Pretend you're visiting from another planet, somehow "dropped" at a zoo. Write a letter that you'll, in alien style, transmit back to your world and tell about the creatures (people and animals) that you've seen.

Write at least 200 words.

Date _____ Title _____

_____

_____

_____

_____

_____

_____

_____

_____

_____

_____

_____

_____

_____

_____

_____

_____

Continued on page _____

More Wild Creatures

Flip through some magazines, and find one picture of a person and another of an animal. *National Geographic* magazine is a great place to find animal pictures. Cut out the figures and place them together so that you have the body of a human and the head of a creature. You might connect a photo of a fashion model to a sea turtle. You may want to blend the body of a baseball player with the head of a peacock.

Spend five minutes contemplating the personality of this new being. When you're ready, create a plot with this character as the protagonist, the star of your story, right here in your journal.

Date _____   Title _____

_____

_____

_____

_____

_____

_____

_____

_____

_____

_____

_____

_____

_____

Continued on page _____

What Would Abby Say?

Go online to visit "Dear Abby," or check it out in your local newspaper. Take one of the letters to Abby and write your response. Be wild, be serious, be funny, and pretend you're the relationship columnist.

Write 200 words.

Having fun, write another response to one of Abby's questions.

Date _____   Title _____

_____

_____

_____

_____

_____

_____

_____

_____

_____

_____

_____

_____

_____

_____

_____

_____

Continued on page _____

Check the Obits

Get a copy of your city or town's newspaper, the print or the electronic version. Select an obituary and read it thoroughly. Put it away for a few hours or even overnight. Now read it again, and see what creative thoughts are stirred. Your goal here is to write a story based on some aspect of the obituary.

Fictionalize all you want, or rewrite the event as an informational article or essay. This exercise should fill up this page and the next. However, why not make it last for a year? You can repeat it every day when you open the morning paper.

Date _____ Title _____

_____

_____

_____

_____

_____

_____

_____

_____

_____

_____

_____

_____

_____

_____

_____

_____

Continued on page _____

Drive-By Writing

Sit in your car and think about a road trip or a place you've driven to. It can be that drive to Walmart when you met up with a high school friend or the time you went to the dry cleaners and came home with the wrong clothing. Or what of that transcontinental adventure when you were just out of college and had to call home for $50 so that you could put gas in the old VW bus?

Spend at least ten minutes thinking of this driven memory, and then write an essay about the experience. Ponder your memories for a while; then choose one to write about.

- Stay focused on your message.

- Add thoughtful, funny, colorful examples.

- Don't tell the mundane details.

- Make the message universal to reach a wide readership.

- Arrive at a basic truth.

- Get your reader involved—ask a question.

- Use emotions and word pictures.

- Pick an experience you care about.

- Steer clear of anger and negative emotions.

- Reveal yourself.

- Use the essay to educate, inform, and entertain.

Date _____ Title _____

_____

_____

_____

_____

_____

_____

_____

_____

_____

_____

_____

_____

_____

_____

_____

_____

_____

_____

_____

_____

_____

_____

_____

_____

_____

Continued on page _____

Teachers Learn, Learners Teach

Write about your most memorable teacher. Did he/she influence you to become the person you are? Was the teacher's effect on you the opposite? Who was the first teacher you remember? Was it perhaps your grandfather or your sister?

How have your actions taught others?

Describe the person or your experience. Include as much dialogue as you can. You may not remember this teacher's exact words, but use the words you can gather from your memory.

You can also fictionalize the memory.

Finally, finish with what you'd say to this teacher if you met today. Write at least 200 words.

Date _____ Title _____

_____

_____

_____

_____

_____

_____

_____

_____

_____

_____

_____

_____

_____

_____

_____

_____

_____

_____

_____

_____

_____

_____

_____

_____

_____

_____

_____

_____

_____

_____

_____

_____

_____

_____

_____

_____

_____

_____

_____

_____

_____

_____   *Continued on page* _____

Powerful Advice? Think Twice

Have you ever given advice to a friend or your children and suddenly you realize your parents used those very words? We've all done that. Have you ever given guidance only to have everything go wrong for the person you've instructed? Have you provided counsel and then seen someone fail?

And what about the opposite? Have you helped or instructed someone and they've succeeded beyond their and your wildest dreams?

People influence our lives. Some for the better. Others have the opposite effect. Think of someone who affected you in some way. It needn't be a life-changing experience.

Did a boss fire you from a job—a job you weren't at all suited for—and did you realize later it was for the best? Did a parent or sibling teach you a skill, such as model building, knitting, or golfing, that has brought you joy? Was there a parent or older adult whose negative role modeling helped decide your own values?

You may want to select someone who was instrumental in a significant life experience, such as a birth, graduation, wedding, death, or religious experience.

Write at least 200 words on a powerful, influential experience.

Date _____ Title _____

_____

_____

_____

_____

_____

_____

Continued on page _____

Sweet Spot

In fifty words or fewer, describe your favorite place on the planet. Choose a place you really love. Write about your hometown or about the region where you live. You can write about the place where you took your last vacation.

Be flowery or serious, but you may not use the following words: pretty, attractive, good, nice, beautiful, lovely, or other wishy-washy descriptive words, and steer clear of very, really, especially, quite, or incredible.

Write a minimum of 200 words.

Date _____ Title _____

_____

_____

_____

_____

_____

_____

_____

_____

_____

_____

_____

_____

_____

_____

_____

_____

Continued on page _____

Assemble This

Draw lines between the most unlikely combination of the following words, and then create an essay, story, or poem using the nouns and modifiers. You can mix and match and twist things around.

Nouns	Modifiers
bagel	wet
pooch	tight-lipped
cornflake	fluffy
catwalk	dusty
golfer	plump
cucumber	rusted
tornado	bleached
robot	squashy
snow	winged
éclair	downy
pinecone	delicate
ballet shoes	tiny
mustang	menacing
elevator	mind-numbing
tile	ulcerated
book	kaput
sister	petrified

bathtub	battered
galaxy	wrestled
cobweb	sterile
tennis shoe	spotless
pliers	untainted
java	mud-spattered
peanut	brawny
coverlet	encrusted
hamburger	saccharine

No one is expecting Pulitzer Prize–winning poetry, but make your goal to increase your creativity. Use the adjoining page and the extra pages at the back to assemble more essays, stories, or poems. This is a simple, highly creative exercise that could spark fresh ideas in all your writing.

Date _____   Title _____

_____

_____

_____

_____

_____

_____

_____

_____

Continued on page _____

Retell the Tale

Take the children's story *Jack and the Beanstalk*, and retell it in a strictly modern way. Give your story a twist, do unexpected things with details. Don't forget to show (by their behavior) the personalities of your characters; don't just tell about them.

The use of dialogue is an excellent way for characters' personalities and problems to be revealed and to keep the plot and drama moving along.

Write to fill up a page or a minimum of 400 words.

If you enjoy this challenge, retell stories such as *Little Women*, *Jane Eyre*, *Tarzan*, *Moby Dick*, and other classics.

Date _____ Title _____

_____

_____

_____

_____

_____

_____

_____

_____

_____

_____

_____

_____

_____

Continued on page _____

Bring Lesser Characters to Life

Have you ever read a book and found a lesser character, who is not the protagonist, to be fascinating? Have you ever wanted to write a book from the POV (point of view) of the Tin Man in *The Wizard of Oz*, or Ellen O'Hara (Scarlett's mom) in *Gone with the Wind*? How about a lesser-known person in the Bible, like Elizabeth or Priscilla?

Now's your chance. Do a bit of research on the character. Read about the character from the original text, and then, using the Bubble Method (which will require a separate piece of paper), bubble a story. When you've got the story thought out, write a story on a page here in the workbook/journal.

If you enjoy this challenge, select another bit player from a classic, and create a story putting this character in the leading role.

Date _____ Title _____

_____

_____

_____

_____

_____

_____

_____

_____

_____

_____

_____

Continued on page _____

Turn a Phase, Tell a Story

Start at the top left grouping of words, and work your way through this list. Take one group each day. Use the first word of the group as the first word of your story, and fill one page in your journal.

Use the two remaining words wherever they fit. Don't forget that every story needs a place, a plot, and something to move a plot forward.

muskrat	pigeon	toilet	staple
turnip	voltage	palm	pineapple
handrail	train	evaporate	rayon
key	shaman	ogle	zucchini
lounge	seconds	hush-hush	silver
porch	toe	framed	paper
hug	haircut	teacup	fig
linen	rattletrap	extraterrestrial	tornado
buccaneer	peanut	lavender	bloom
hawk	dumbfound	unseen	writer
petite	pervade	poodle	baloney
laundry	scrubs	dilettante	torrent
cascade	segregate	aficionado	halt
banana	rationale	postcard	iced tea
kid	help	blanket	gloomy
vinegary	charming	sweet	pencil
breakable	deodorant	crutch	smirk
lasagna	London	rove	Goliath
academy	tariffs	dishrag	envelope
burden	blame	pencil	stuff
blue	muffin	pardon	plasma

brut	tumbleweed	unemployment	unwrap
tome	accolade	laser	chocolate
can opener	socks	thumb	statue
shark	leprechaun	bacon	filth
nephew	hard drive	cylinder	steel
pillow	peanut	tiptoe	suffocate
bazaar	stockroom	conductor	fat
horse	lumber	tar	cornice
ogre	manuscript	rain	toast
urchin	praise	tornado	vicar
chicken	help	stair	orange
burnish	mouse	muck	tartlet
iced tea	pinky	cement	olive oil
lunge	ski	kiss	hug
hungry	dumbstruck	perturb	noise
small	wolf	avenue	available
speculate	preacher	hurricane	snail
hot	freak	feather	fuss
comedy	nurse	caterpillar	spider
puss	afternoon	brownie	hearth
squeeze	clap	cuddle	crude
embrace	stoop	handle	monocle
finalize	seal	course	tie
butler	substance	affair	dilemma
danger	hitch	quandary	ornament
coast	villain	quaff	boast
corner	outlook	path	lucid
unequivocal	jet	migraine	turkey
plain	copyright	natural	nude
screening	broadcast	ordeal	paucity

comic	hail	stem	burger
lung	sarcastic	ecstasy	glee
relish	silence	monotonous	dry
cohabitate	sultry	humid	bear
accounts	van	granite	harpy
hoodwink	prisoner	annoy	jeopardy

Date _____ Title _____

_____

_____

_____

_____

_____

_____

_____

_____

_____

_____

_____

_____

_____

_____

_____

_____

Continued on page _____

The Ending as Your Beginning

When you've finished the Writeriffic assignments, please let me know.

I created these assignments for you, and I'd love your feedback.

What inspired your creative writing? What made you want to scream? What did you like? What did you hate?

Let me know, please. I'm working on Writeriffic 3—the third edition—right now, and the suggestions you have just might show up in the next edition of this book.

When I hear from you, you can be sure I'll contact you. Write to me at askeva@evashaw.com or via postal mail at P. O. Box 524, Carlsbad, CA 92018-0524.

Continued from page _____

Continued from page _____

Continued from page _____

Continued from page _____

Continued from page _____

Continued from page _____

Continued from page _____

Continued from page _____

Continued from page _____

Continued from page _____

Continued from page _____

Continued from page _____

Continued from page _____

Continued from page _____

Continued from page _____

Continued from page _____

Continued from page _____

Continued from page _____

Continued from page _____

Continued from page _____

Continued from page _____

Continued from page _____

Continued from page _____

Continued from page _____

Continued from page _____

Continued from page _____

Continued from page _____

Continued from page _____

Continued from page _____

Continued from page _____

Continued from page _____

Continued from page _____

Continued from page _____

Continued from page _____

Continued from page _____

Continued from page _____

Continued from page _____

Continued from page _____

Continued from page _____

Continued from page _____

Continued from page _____

Continued from page _____

Continued from page _____

Continued from page _____

Continued from page _____

Continued from page _____

Continued from page _____

Continued from page _____

Continued from page _____

Continued from page _____

Continued from page _____

Continued from page _____

Continued from page _____

Continued from page _____

Continued from page _____

Continued from page _____

Continued from page _____

Continued from page _____

Continued from page _____

Continued from page _____

Continued from page _____

Continued from page _____

Continued from page _____

Continued from page _____

Continued from page _____

Continued from page _____

Continued from page _____

Continued from page _____

Continued from page _____

Continued from page _____

Continued from page _____

Continued from page _____

Continued from page _____

Continued from page _____

Continued from page _____

Continued from page _____

Continued from page _____

Continued from page _____

Continued from page _____

Continued from page _____

Continued from page _____

Continued from page _____

Continued from page _____

Continued from page _____

Continued from page _____

Continued from page _____

Continued from page _____